CAPTURED
SPORTS
HISTORY

MIRACLE ON ICE

HOW A STUNNING UPSET UNITED A COUNTRY

by Michael Burgan

Content Adviser: John Harrington
Forward, 1980 U.S. National Hockey Team;
Women's Hockey Coach, Minnesota State University, Mankato

COMPASS POINT BOOKS
a capstone imprint

Compass Point Books are published by Capstone,
1710 Roe Crest Drive, North Mankato, Minnesota 56003
www.mycapstone.com

Editor: Catherine Neitge
Designers: Tracy Davies McCabe and Catherine Neitge
Media Researcher: Eric Gohl
Library Consultant: Kathleen Baxter
Production Specialist: Lori Barbeau

Image Credits
Alamy: Moviestore Collection Ltd, 52, 58 (bottom); AP Photo: 11, 56 (top), Douglas
Ball, 28, Mike Groll, 59 (bottom); Bridgeman Images: Gamborg Collection/Rojter,
Mikhail Grigorievich (1916-93), 19; Corbis: Bettmann, 18; Getty Images: B Bennett,
29, 46, 56 (bottom), CNP/Keystone, 44, Focus on Sport, 36, John Kelly, 10, Melchior
DiGiacomo, 23, 24, 25, *Sports Illustrated*/Bill Frakes, 51, *Sports Illustrated*/Eric
Schweikardt, 5, 9, 31, 38, *Sports Illustrated*/Heinz Kluetmeier, cover, 13, 27, 33,
34, 37, 40, 43, 45, 48, 49, 50, 57 (right), 58 (top), 59 (top), Steve Powell, 7, UIG/
Sovfoto, 21, ullstein bild/Horstmüller, 35, WireImage/Jemal Countess, 39; Newscom:
akg-images, 20, Icon SMI/Imago/Sven Simon, 57 (left), Reuters/Steve Wilson, 55,
Universal Images Group/Sovfoto, 15, ZUMA Press/KPA, 17, ZUMA Press/TASS, 22

Library of Congress Cataloging-in-Publication Data
Cataloging-in-publication information is on file with the Library of Congress.
ISBN 978-0-7565-5290-9 (library binding)
ISBN 978-0-7565-5294-7 (paperback)
ISBN 978-0-7565-5298-5 (ebook PDF)

Printed in the United States of America, in Stevens Point Wisconsin.
092015   009222WZS16

TABLEOFCONTENTS

ChapterOne
WORKING TOWARD AN UPSET

With the score tied 3-3 in the third period, the United States hockey team changed its forward line. Mike Eruzione stepped onto the rink and chased after a puck his teammates John Harrington and Mark Pavelich had dumped into center ice. Eruzione was the captain of the U.S. team, which was playing the Soviet Union in a crucial semifinal game at the 1980 Winter Olympics. If Team USA won this February 22 contest, it would have a chance to play for the gold medal. Cheering on the Americans was an enthusiastic crowd of about 10,000 people jammed into the small ice arena at Lake Placid, New York.

But what were the odds Eruzione and the young Americans could beat the mighty Soviet team, which had won the last four Olympic gold medals in hockey? At that time Olympic athletes had to be amateurs. Many of the Soviet players belonged to their country's army, the Red Army, so technically they were paid as soldiers, not athletes. But the whole world knew they were selected, trained, and paid to play hockey for their country. Most of the Soviet players were in their mid-to-late 20s, while a few were just over 30. They had years of international experience playing together as a team.

Their experience and skill made the Soviet players among the best in the world. Just the year before, in a series played in New York, the Soviets had taken two out

But what were the odds Eruzione and the young Americans could beat the mighty Soviet team, which had won the last four Olympic gold medals in hockey?

Team captain Mike Eruzione sped down the ice at the Lake Placid Olympic Arena.

of three games from the National Hockey League (NHL) All-Stars. The Red Army team won the final game against the NHLers with its best goalie, Vladislav Tretiak, sitting on the bench. But even with Soviet backup goalie Vladimir Myshkin in the net, the All-Stars could not score a goal.

The Americans, on the other hand, were mostly college students. While they excelled at their sport in school, they had started training and playing international hockey together only a few months before the 1980 Games. The selection process to create Team USA began with its coach, Herb Brooks, who was also the hockey coach at the University of Minnesota. Brooks wanted players who would work hard and not crack under stress. Nine of the players he chose had been with him at Minnesota. He knew their talents, and they knew his coaching style.

Mike Eruzione, 25, a left winger, was one of the oldest players on the squad. He was one of four players from Massachusetts. The rest were from the Midwest—12 from Minnesota and two each from Wisconsin and Michigan. Those states were the hotbeds of U.S. amateur hockey, but the American presence in the NHL was still fairly small. Only about 12 percent of the pro players were American, in a league dominated by Canadians. Compared with professional baseball, football, and basketball, hockey interested few U.S. sports fans.

Eruzione was one of the players who had done well in college, setting scoring records at Boston University. In the games leading up to the Olympics, however, he had trouble scoring, and at one point Coach Brooks decided to cut him from the team. Brooks told his friend Gus Hendrickson, another college coach, that he planned to dump Eruzione. "But Eruzione's your leader," Hendrickson said. "You need a leader." The other players were upset when they heard they might lose their captain. Everyone knew Eruzione was not the best scorer or skater on the team. But they also saw that he was a leader, someone who could boost their spirits and encourage them to play harder. Brooks finally saw that cutting Eruzione would not be good for the team, and so he let him stay.

Compared with professional baseball, football, and basketball, hockey interested few U.S. sports fans.

Future four-time NHL All-Star Mike Ramsey (top) checked a West German player during Team USA's road to the Olympic medal round.

The youngest player on the team was defenseman Mike Ramsey. He had just turned 19 a few months before the Olympics. Despite his youth, he was a star for the Americans. In 1979 he was the first American college player ever taken in the first round of the NHL draft. Several of his teammates had also been drafted, but they, like Ramsey, chose to delay professional careers to play for Team USA.

One drafted player who decided to play for Brooks instead was defenseman Ken Morrow. He was large and strong, and his full beard made him stand out among his mostly clean-shaven teammates. Morrow held off playing for the New York Islanders so he could go to the Olympics.

Like Morrow and Ramsey, Mark Johnson was talented enough to play in the NHL. The center played for his father, Bob Johnson, at the University of Wisconsin. Known as "Badger Bob," Mark's father had coached the 1976 Olympic team. He had almost chosen Mark to play for him, even though his son was then only 17. By 1979 Brooks knew he wanted Mark Johnson as his top center. He told Johnson that the team needed him if it was going to advance through the Olympics.

The team also needed the gutsy goalie, Jim Craig. Filled with confidence, Craig was known for his quick glove hand and his constant chatter during a game. Teammates tried to ignore a lot of what he said—especially if he was criticizing their play. Craig had allowed an average of only 2.37 goals per game in the 48 games he played for Team USA before the Olympics.

Craig played well in Team USA's first game of the 1980 Olympics on February 12, giving up only two goals against Sweden. His teammates, though, struggled offensively, and with only a minute to play, the Americans were in danger of losing the game 2-1. To add extra offense, Coach Brooks pulled Craig from the net and added a sixth attacker. As the clock wound down, Buzz Schneider, the

Buzz Schneider celebrated after scoring a goal against Czechoslovakia, one of the world's best teams.

only player returning from the 1976 Olympic team, passed to defenseman Bill Baker, and his slap shot from just inside Sweden's blue line found the net. Since the teams did not play overtime in the round-robin games, Team USA earned a tie and a point in the standings.

After that close call, the Americans went on a roll. First they beat a well-regarded team from Czechoslovakia,

7-3. Ken Morrow called it "the best game we played in the tournament." It gave the players confidence that they could compete with the world's best teams. Team USA then defeated Norway and Romania. Their fifth game was against West Germany, which had knocked the Americans out of the medal round in 1976. After falling behind the Germans 2-0, the Americans scored four straight goals, including two by left winger Rob McClanahan, one of the players from the University of Minnesota. With that win, Team USA reached the medal round. Their next opponent: the mighty Red Army team of the Soviet Union.

Tension had filled the Lake Placid Olympic Arena since the opening face-off. Fans sat or stood tightly together, because the crowd was several thousand people larger than what the arena was built to hold. Now, in a tie game against the sport's greatest team, Mike Eruzione took the puck in a play set up by Harrington and Pavelich. Eruzione launched a shot at Soviet goalie Vladimir Myshkin. At almost the same time, a Soviet defenseman dropped to his knees on the ice to try to block the shot. The puck shot past him and flew toward Myshkin, who had trouble seeing it. In an instant, the puck was in the net, and Eruzione was celebrating the goal that gave the Americans their first lead of the game. It was also the first time a U.S. team had held a lead over any Soviet team in the Olympics since 1960. Now the Americans and their fans wondered: Could they keep that lead?

Goalie Jim Craig blocked a shot during the game against the Soviets, one of 36 saves.

THE 1960 OLYMPICS

Roger and Bill Christian (from left) teamed up for two goals during the 1960 win against the Soviets.

Team USA and the Soviet team had squared off in another important game 20 years before their match in Lake Placid. In the 1960 Olympic Games, the two teams played to see who would compete for the gold. The Soviet team was on its way to becoming a powerhouse team, having won the gold medal at the previous games. The Americans had never beaten them in hockey competition. The Americans had won the silver medal in the 1956 Games, but they were not expected to do well in 1960, even though they were playing before a home crowd in Squaw Valley, California.

But Team USA made it to the medal round and a game against the Soviets. The hero of the game was Bill Christian, who scored twice, with his brother Roger assisting on each play. The final score was 3-2, and the Americans then went on to beat Czechoslovakia to win the gold medal.

The 1980 U.S. team had some connections to the 1960 team. Before the Squaw Valley Games, future coach Herb Brooks was the last player cut from the roster. And Dave Christian, who played defense for Brooks in 1980, was the son of Bill Christian.

For the next 10 minutes, the Soviets pressed hard on offense, trying to get a tying goal. Craig played well, turning away shots, but luck helped him when Aleksandr Maltsev hit a goal post with one shot and missed a partly open net with another. The American defensemen tried to block as many shots as they could, and Craig tried not to freeze the puck. He didn't want a face-off near his net. He wanted the clock to keep running down and stop the Soviets from setting up a play. As the action went on, Herb Brooks called out from behind the bench, "Play your game! Play your game!" And in the stands, the American fans chanted their encouragement: "U-S-A, U-S-A."

The Americans knew the Soviets could come from behind to win—they had done it in the teams' last two games. But this time the Soviets could not produce any heroics. As the clocked ticked off the minutes, then the seconds, it was clear that Team USA was going to pull off one of the greatest upsets in the history of sports.

On a platform above the action, TV announcer Al Michaels watched the clock, as well as the skaters on the ice. Just before the horn sounded to end the game, he asked his audience, "Do you believe in miracles? Yes!" In front of his goal, Jim Craig leapt into the air, and soon his teammates raced toward him as they all celebrated their historic victory. At that instant, sports photographer Heinz Kluetmeier snapped a picture of the joyous moment, with fans waving a U.S. flag in the background. The photo soon became almost as well known as the Americans' stunning upset.

"Do you believe in miracles? Yes!"

Heinz Kluetmeier's iconic photo captured the joy of the Miracle on Ice.

The game between Team USA and the Soviet Union was not broadcast live in the United States, but millions of Americans heard Michaels' question about miracles several hours later when they watched it on tape delay. The viewers, like the people in the Olympic Arena, witnessed the Miracle on Ice.

ChapterTwo
COLD WAR SPORTS

The game between the Americans and the Soviets in Lake Placid was about more than hockey. Sporting events between the two countries had taken on extra meaning since the 1950s, when the Cold War gripped the world.

During World War II, the Americans and Soviets had worked together with other allies to defeat Germany. The two countries, however, distrusted each other. The U.S. economy was built on capitalism. People had freedom to invest their money as they chose, own businesses, and try to amass as much wealth as they could. Going along with that economic system was a democratic political system—it called for free elections to choose government leaders at all levels.

The Soviet Union was founded after the 1917 Russian revolution as a communist state. The economy was based on the government's owning most property and businesses. The government was controlled by the Communist Party, which did not allow other parties to participate. To ensure their rule, the Communists clamped down on free speech. They arrested—and often killed or banished to faraway parts of the country, like wintry Siberia—people who opposed their rule.

One goal of the Soviet Communists was to spread their form of government and economic system to as many countries as possible. After World War II, the Soviet Union

Soviet missiles were on display during a 1960s parade in Moscow's Red Square. The communist Soviet Union formed in 1922 when Russia combined with 14 other republics in Eastern Europe and Central Asia. It broke apart in 1991.

extended its totalitarian system over parts of Eastern Europe. The Cold War was about the Soviets' wanting to protect those gains and continue to spread communism. U.S. leaders saw this effort as a threat to capitalism and democracy and wanted to confront the Soviet Union.

The war between the two superpowers was a "cold" one because they did not engage in active combat against each other. Instead, they supported other nations or political groups that believed in either communism or capitalism. These groups battled each other around the world, most notably during the Korean and Vietnam wars.

For a time after World War II, Soviet leaders did not want their athletes to compete against athletes from capitalist nations unless they were assured of victory. But in 1951 the Soviet Union joined the International Olympic Committee (IOC). Soviet athletes were already mostly soldiers and police officers who received pay while they trained for their sports. If they won important events or set world records, the government rewarded them with such things as money or new cars. The situation was similar in the Eastern European nations that the Soviet Union controlled. Meanwhile, U.S. Olympic athletes of this time were true amateurs, though hockey players could play in minor leagues outside of the NHL that offered some pay. (Mike Eruzione, for example, played for the Toledo Goaldiggers before joining Team USA.)

Soviet leaders wanted to prove that communism was better than capitalism. They believed that one way to do so was to support their athletes so they could defeat the Americans whenever possible. Soviet success on the sports field might also turn people's attention away from a distressing fact: Communism deprived Soviet citizens of their freedom and kept most of them poor.

The mingling of sports achievements and political ideology didn't start with the Soviets. In 1936 Adolph Hitler wanted to use the Summer Olympics in Berlin to highlight what he considered Germany's "master race." He also wanted to create a better image for his country across the world, trying to show that it was a peaceful

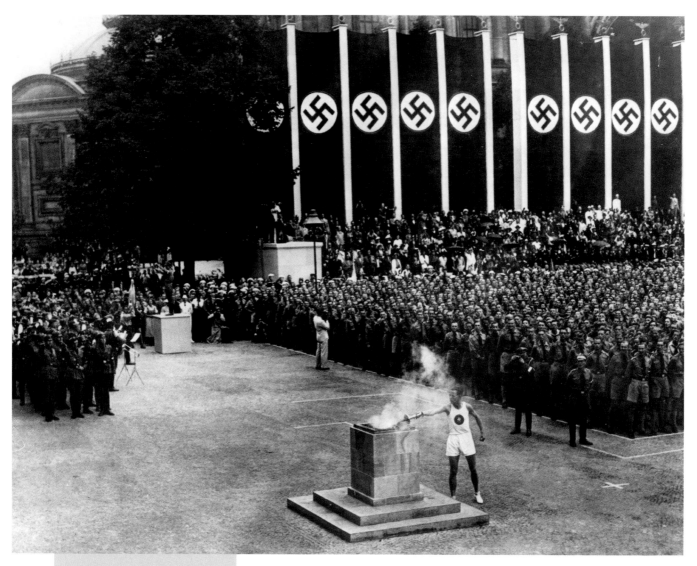

Nazi banners were prominently on display at the 1936 Summer Olympics in Berlin, Germany.

country that treated everyone fairly. In reality, Hitler was already building a huge military to carry out attacks on neighboring countries. His government was also throwing political enemies into prison camps and discriminating against Jews. But as Frederick Birchall of *The New York Times* reported in August 1936, Germany's efforts to show a positive side to Hitler's rule worked. "The strongest impression that visitors will carry away," Birchall wrote,

An official tended to Hungarian water polo player Erwin Zador. The athlete was bloodied by a Soviet player during a match at the 1956 Summer Games.

"is the sense of having experienced exceeding courtesy, extreme consideration and hospitality organized to the last degree."

Politics and sports also could lead to violence, as happened during the 1956 Summer Games in Melbourne, Australia. Before the games began, Soviet troops had gone into Hungary to violently end a rebellion against Communist rule. When water polo players from the two countries met in the Olympic semifinals, they kicked, hit, and scratched each other. One Soviet player threw a punch that drew a Hungarian's blood. The violence was in part a reaction to the military events unfolding in Europe.

Bandy, a 1958 lithograph by prominent Russian artist Mikhail Rojter

Hungary was declared the winner and eventually took the gold medal.

Violence—on or off the ice—was not a factor in Soviet hockey. The Soviet Union was a newcomer to the sport, at least as it had been played in North America for decades. Young Russians enjoyed a game called bandy, which was played outside on huge rinks. Players passed a small ball rather than a puck, and goalies defended the net with just their gloved hands. The game has been compared to soccer on ice. But changes came to the Soviet Union after World War II, when legendary coach Anatoly Tarasov visited Canada and watched athletes playing hockey on smaller indoor rinks. Tarasov promoted Canadian-style hockey and became known as the father of hockey in the Soviet Union. But he adapted the game so that Soviet players

relied more on fast skating and crisp passing than forceful checks and other aggressive contact common in the NHL. The Soviet skaters took their time setting up plays and finding holes in the defense. The North American game was more about dump and chase—the team with the puck dumped it into the defensive team's zone, then chased after it. The offensive team tried to tie up the defenders along the boards and then set up a shot on goal.

Tarasov believed in training hard, and his players lifted weights and ran long distances before it was common for most American athletes. The Soviet players also took dance lessons to improve their balance on the ice. Tarasov

The Canadians and Americans played North American-style hockey at the 1932 Winter Games at Lake Placid. Canada won the gold and the U.S. took silver.

Famed coach Anatoly Tarasov (right) with future Olympic goalie Vladislav Tretiak

wanted his players to plan their moves strategically. He once said a hockey player "must have the wisdom of a chess player, the accuracy of a sniper and the rhythm of a musician." But more important, he said, "he must be a superb athlete." The players also had to make quick decisions on the ice, reacting to what their opponents did.

Tarasov needed less than 10 years to make the Soviet Union an international power in hockey. The country won the International Ice Hockey Federation championship in 1954 and its first Olympic gold medal two years later. By the end of the decade, hockey was the sport that seemed

to offer the best proof, at least to the Soviets, that their country had the best political and economic system. Hockey officials held tryouts for young boys across the country, seeking the best talent. Tarasov wrote books on how to play hockey, and young players read them closely. Vyacheslav "Slava" Fetisov, who played for the Soviet team in 1980, said, "His books were laid next to my bed since I was a little kid. He described the game in a very simple way."

An early goal of Tarasov's was for his team to play against the best Canadian players. He suggested it to Soviet officials in 1964, but they said no, fearing that their players would lose. The match finally took place in

The Soviets won two of the first four Summit Series games and tied another before heading to Moscow to play four more games against the Canadian professionals.

1972, though Tarasov was no longer coaching the Soviet team. That year Canada and the Soviet Union played eight games—four in Canada and four in the Soviet Union—in what was called the Summit Series. Although the Soviets were good at international hockey, the Canadian professionals expected to dominate. Instead, in a series that highlighted the different styles of play, the Canadians scrambled to win the last three games—played in the Soviet capital of Moscow—to win the series.

The Soviet players surprised the Canadians with their hockey expertise during the Summit Series, which began in Montreal.

Soviet forward Aleksandr Maltsev (10), who would go on to play in the 1980 Olympics, battled for the puck during the 1972 Summit Series.

"We didn't take them seriously," said Toronto Maple Leafs forward Paul Henderson. "We knew they were good hockey players. But the lineup we had—how could we ever lose?"

Several Soviet players from that series faced the Americans in Lake Placid in 1980. Given their talent, the Soviets might have asked themselves the same question.

Something was different about the Soviet opponent, though. Herb Brooks was taking a new approach to the game—new for the Americans, anyway. He wanted to get rid of the dump-and-chase style and play more like the Soviets. He had played against the teams Tarasov had coached and had even asked him about the Soviets' style of play. Brooks' American team would try to copy the training that helped Soviet players keep their energy the entire game. His players would stress accurate passing and keeping control of the puck, as the Soviets did. The Americans would not give up delivering powerful checks when the situation called for it. Even the Soviets had adopted some of the more physical play of the NHL. But Brooks wanted to use Soviet methods to try to beat them.

In the summer of 1979 Brooks brought 68 amateur players, most in college, to a training camp in Colorado Springs, Colorado. He wanted fast and talented players, of course, but also men who would work well together as a team. This was important, since most players on the final roster came from New England and the Midwest and had competed fiercely against each other in college. Sportswriter Wayne Coffey said Brooks had an unusual strategy right from the start: "He would make himself the enemy." That, he thought, would unite the players against him. Brooks did that by holding brutal practices and always demanding more. "I'm not here to be your friend," Brooks told the team. "I'm here to be your coach." He later called it his loneliest year in hockey.

"I'm not here to be your friend," Brooks told the team. "I'm here to be your coach."

HALL OF FAME COACH

Heinz Kluetmeier photographed Herb Brooks during the 1980 gold-medal game against Finland.

Like many young hockey players in Minnesota, Herb Brooks dreamed of becoming an NHL star. Instead he became one of the greatest coaches the game has ever seen. A talented high school hockey player, Brooks went on to play at the University of Minnesota. He was chosen for several U.S. national teams, including the 1964 and 1968 Olympic teams.

When he stopped playing, Brooks turned to coaching, first at the university. He led the Minnesota team to three national championships before taking over the 1980 Olympic team. Along with demanding that the Olympians play hard, he was known to amuse the players with expressions they called "Herbie-isms." One famous example was "You don't have enough talent to win on talent alone." Another was "You're playing worse every day, and right now you're playing like it's next month."

Brooks' success at Lake Placid cemented his reputation as one of the great hockey coaches of the day. After the Olympics, Brooks coached for several NHL and college hockey teams. Coaching the New York Rangers during the 1981–82 season, he directed the team to a 39-27-14 record and was named NHL Coach of the Year. Brooks returned to Olympic hockey in 2002. He coached Team USA to the silver medal at the Winter Games in Salt Lake City, Utah. Brooks was killed in a car accident the next year. He was inducted into the Hockey Hall of Fame in 2006.

Brooks (left) coached his young players on the ice during vigorous practice sessions before the Olympic Games.

After their rigorous training, the 26 Americans selected for the national team set off on a 61-game pre-Olympics schedule. (The roster would be cut to 20 before the start of the Lake Placid Games.) They played several NHL teams, college teams, and foreign teams. Going into their last game, on February 9, 1980, at New York's Madison Square Garden, the team had a record of 42-15-3. But the opponent in that last warm-up game presented a different kind of challenge. The Americans faced the mighty Soviet team.

Before the game Brooks told his team to have fun—not something he usually said. As the game went on, some of the Americans were in awe of the Soviets, who raced out

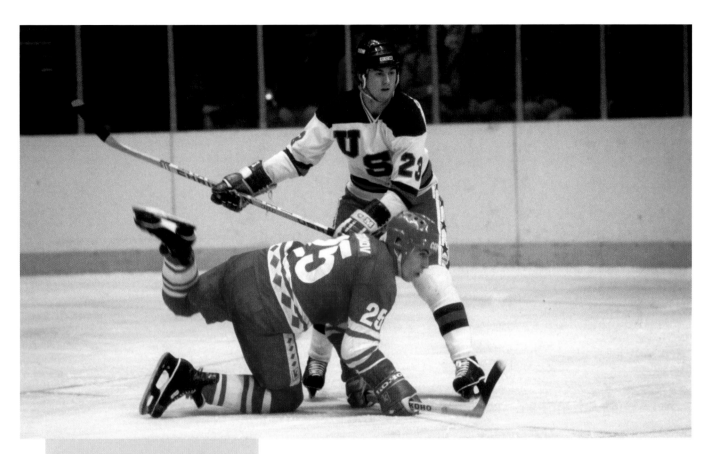

Dave Christian of Team USA and Vladimir Golikov of the Soviet Union battled it out at Madison Square Garden in the final game before the Winter Olympics.

to a 4-0 lead at the end of the first period. The final score: 10-3, in favor of the Soviets. The result, the *New York Daily News* reported, "came as no surprise" given "the swiftness, precision and ruthlessness" of the Soviet team.

After the game Soviet coach Viktor Tikhonov said his team could have scored even more goals if it had wanted to. What Tikhonov and others didn't realize was that Brooks was not eager that day to show the Soviets all his team could do. The Americans would save their best for the Olympics.

ChapterThree
UNITING A NATION

When the Americans and Soviets met before the Olympics in Madison Square Garden, Cold War politics seemed ready to shape another Olympics. In December 1979 the Soviet Union had invaded Afghanistan to support a Communist-leaning government there that it could easily control. The United States opposed the Soviet action but was not ready to get directly involved. Still, President Jimmy Carter wanted to show U.S. displeasure. He announced limits on trade with the Soviet Union. On January 20 he said that if the Soviet military did not leave Afghanistan, the International Olympic Committee should move, postpone, or cancel the 1980 Summer Olympics. Those games were going to be held in Moscow. If the games weren't canceled or moved, Carter said, the United States should boycott the games.

Congress backed the president's call for a boycott. The United States Olympic Committee (USOC) would make the final decision on whether to send U.S. athletes to the Moscow Games. That decision would not come until the spring. But Carter put pressure on the committee. If it didn't boycott the Summer Games, he said, the U.S. government would cut off funding for training and would tax other USOC income.

When the Winter Games started, the political atmosphere was not on the minds of the U.S. hockey team.

The players and their coach were focused on winning. The Soviet players, though, may have felt more of the tension. They traveled with even more security agents than usual. As player Sergei Makarov explained, Soviet officials "were afraid that someone would do something to us." But off the ice, nothing happened. The real tension and conflict came on the ice, especially in the semifinal game.

Although the Americans had played well throughout the games, no one knew what to expect from the matchup with the Soviets. Would the Americans face another drubbing, like the 10-3 loss just before the games? Or would they at least give the Soviets a good challenge? Winning the game, most experts believed, was beyond the Americans' reach.

Herb Brooks had a different opinion. His players knew the importance of the game against the Soviet team. But he wanted them to know that he believed in them and their skills. In the locker room before the game, he said, "You were born to be a player. You were meant to be here. This moment is yours." The coach who had worked his players so hard in practice, and who sometimes barely spoke to them, said perhaps the most famous words of his life—and his players responded.

The game began at 5:06 p.m. It was broadcast live in Canada but not in the United States. The ABC television network recorded the game to show that night during prime time. The first period started with both goalies making good saves. But about halfway through the period, the Soviets forced a turnover in the American zone, and soon the puck was under Jim Craig's glove for the first score. The Americans got the goal back a few minutes later when Buzz Schneider launched a slap shot from about 40 feet (12 meters) out.

A lucky bounce helped the Soviets score their next goal. As Sergei Makarov tried to pass to a teammate, the puck bounced off Ken Morrow's skate and right back to Makarov, who was alone in front of Craig. He fired a hard, fast shot into the net to make the score 2-1.

"You were born to be a player. You were meant to be here. This moment is yours."

Vladimir Krutov scored the first goal of the game, slipping the puck past U.S. goalie Jim Craig.

The Soviet team had been playing with its usual crisp style. But as the first period was about to end, Dave Christian took a long shot on goal. Goalie Vladislav Tretiak stopped the puck, but it bounced out toward Mark Johnson, who had just come on the ice after one last line change. The Russian defensemen were already heading toward the bench. "Everybody thought the period was over," one of them later said. "We were all watching the clock. It was just a few seconds left." But there was enough time for Johnson to race by the Soviet defenders, pick up the puck, and beat Tretiak in close for the tying goal.

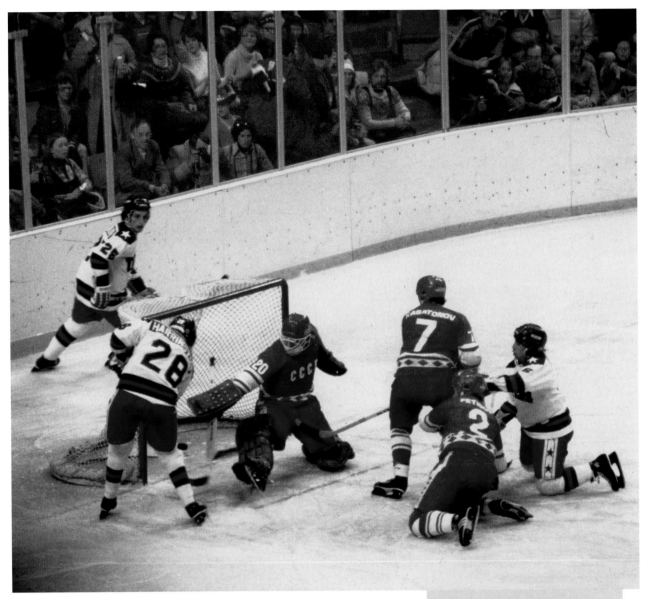

When the second period started, the Americans were surprised to see Vladimir Myshkin in the Soviet net. Although skilled, he was not as good as Tretiak, who later said, "It was difficult for me to sit on the bench with the score 2-2." The superstar goalie wanted to be on the ice during this critical time. But perhaps Soviet coach Viktor Tikhonov was angry because Tretiak had allowed the

Vladislav Tretiak, considered the best goalie in the world, had six saves during the first period. The decision to bench him was shocking to players and fans.

TIKHONOV'S BLUNDER

The decision to bench star goalie Vladislav Tretiak haunted famed coach Viktor Tikhonov (left).

To Soviet players and hockey experts, the biggest play of the Miracle on Ice game might have happened off the ice. They did not understand why Soviet coach Viktor Tikhonov had replaced goalie Vladislav Tretiak with Vladimir Myshkin. After the game, the team's assistant coach, Vladimir Jursinov, offered an explanation: "He is not playing well and my feeling is he is nervous." But would the man many considered the world's greatest goalie feel nervous about playing college students? Soviet player Sergei Makarov later said, "Tikhonov was panicking. He couldn't control himself. That's what it was—panic." The move upset all the Soviet players. Years later, Mark Johnson was an NHL teammate of Slava Fetisov. Johnson asked the great defenseman what had happened with the goalie replacement. Speaking in very basic English, Fetisov replied, "Coach crazy." Long after the games, Tikhonov admitted he had gotten angry when Tretiak gave up the last-second goal. "My blood was boiling," he said. Pulling Tretiak, he said, "was my worst mistake, my biggest regret."

last-second goal. Or maybe he thought the team needed
a jolt. In either case, Myshkin shut out the Americans
during the second period, and the Soviets regained the
lead on a goal by Aleksandr Maltsev.

At the start of the third period, the Americans could
barely move the puck toward the net. For the first seven
minutes, Myshkin faced only two shots on goal. The
Americans also seemed to waste a two-minute power
play, but at the last second, the puck bounced off a Soviet

player's skate and onto Mark Johnson's stick. The center, nicknamed Magic, fired in his second goal, tying the score.

The arena erupted with cheers, shaking the building. Less than 90 seconds later, Team USA gave the fans something else to roar about. John Harrington went into the Soviet end for the puck near the boards, and it bounced out to Mark Pavelich. Falling as he got the puck, Pavelich passed it toward the center of the rink. A speeding Mike Eruzione got the puck and shot it into

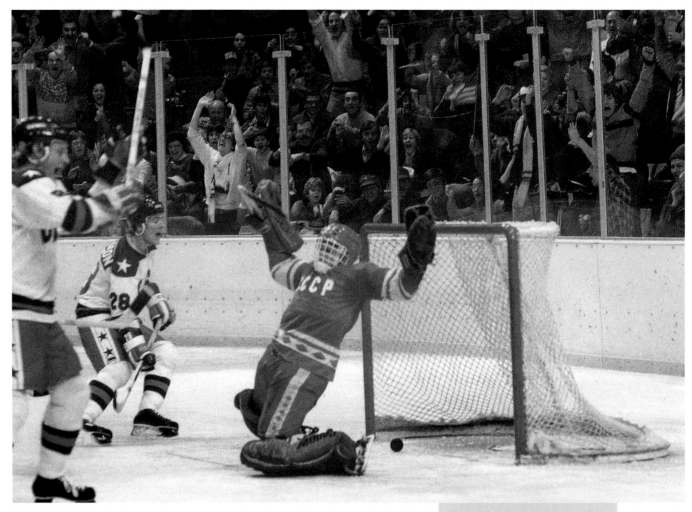

Goalie Vladimir Myshkin couldn't stop Mike Eruzione's goal, which gave Team USA its miraculous win.

the Soviet net for the goal that gave the Americans the improbable 4-3 lead. They kept the lead to the end of the game.

In the overflow crowd that evening were journalists and photographers from around the world. One of them was Heinz Kluetmeier, a photographer for *Sports Illustrated*. Born in Germany, Kluetmeier had come to the United States with his family in 1952. By that time, his native country had been divided into eastern and western halves, with East Germany under Soviet control and West

Photographer Heinz Kluetmeier has received many honors during his long career.

Germany loyal to the United States. When he arrived in the United States, Kluetmeier knew only a few words of English.

His photography career began while he was in high school, taking pictures of football games and other events for the Associated Press (AP). During college summer breaks he continued to work for the AP, and he also shot photos for the *Milwaukee Journal* and *Life* magazine. A few years after graduating with an engineering degree, he became a professional photographer, joining Time Inc. and shooting photos for *Sports Illustrated* and *Life*. In 1972 he covered his first Olympics, the Summer Games in Munich, Germany. Those games had a political angle too, one that turned deadly. Palestinians who wanted to undermine Israel sometimes carried out terrorist attacks. In Munich, Palestinian terrorists kidnapped Israeli athletes, and the resulting violence killed 17 people.

For the 1980 U.S.-Soviet hockey game, Kluetmeier considered shooting the action from a place close to the ice. The rink, though, was surrounded by large sheets of thick plastic that protected fans from flying pucks. Not wanting to shoot through the plastic, Kluetmeier stood on a platform with an ABC cameraman.

As the last seconds ticked off, Kluetmeier aimed his camera at the U.S goal. When the horn sounded to end the game, the American players raced toward the net and goalie Jim Craig. The players threw their arms into the air, fell to the ice, and hugged each other. In the

Kluetmeier's photo on the cover of *Sports Illustrated* needed no words to describe it.

stands, fans waved American flags. As the celebration went on, Kluetmeier clicked away. One of his pictures soon appeared on the cover of *Sports Illustrated*. The magazine's editors did not use any headline or other words to describe the scene. By then, the whole country

His Miracle on Ice photo defined a moment when Americans could forget about their problems and celebrate a great and unexpected victory.

knew that the image represented the Americans' Miracle on Ice.

Years later, Kluetmeier described what made a great photograph. It's one, he said, that "defines a moment in the world, in an event and in life that people go back to again and again." His Miracle on Ice photo defined a moment when Americans could forget about their problems and celebrate a great and unexpected victory. The Soviet invasion of Afghanistan showed how dangerous the Cold War still was. At home, Americans had faced a tough economy for several years. The victory at Lake Placid united Americans as nothing in recent years had. The win stirred pride across the country, even in people who were not usually hockey fans. Some had never watched a hockey game before, but as Al Michaels said, "That was the beauty of that game. You didn't have to understand to understand."

In the moments after seeing or hearing about the victory, Americans across the country cheered and hugged, just as the players had. In Lake Placid, fireworks lit the winter sky. President Carter called Brooks to congratulate him and the team. Brooks told reporters, "He said we had made the American people very proud, and reflected the ideals of the country." But as Americans celebrated the victory, the players knew they had one more game to play.

ChapterFour
A GOLDEN MOMENT AND BEYOND

All the happiness, excitement, and pride that Team USA generated on February 22, 1980, could not hide one fact: They still had to win one more game to earn the gold medal and complete the miracle. Two days later the players stepped onto the Lake Placid ice to face Finland. If they won, the gold was theirs. If they lost, and depending on what happened in a game between Sweden and the Soviet Union, they might not win any medal.

As they did against the Soviet Union, the Americans fell behind in the first period, 1-0. They tied it on a Steve Christoff goal in the second period, but the Finns quickly scored again on a power play. The Americans entered the third period trailing 2-1. Could they come from behind again?

It took only a few minutes for Phil Verchota to tie the score. Then Rob McClanahan made it 3-2 on a shot that went between the Finnish goalie's legs. Once again, all the Americans had to do was keep the lead they had claimed. But they made it hard for themselves, drawing two penalties almost back to back. The short-handed defense rose to the occasion, killing both penalties. Then a ref whistled Verchota for another penalty with about four minutes to play. This time the defense not only shut down the Finns, but Mark Johnson worked his magic again. He caught the puck before it bounced out of the Finns' zone,

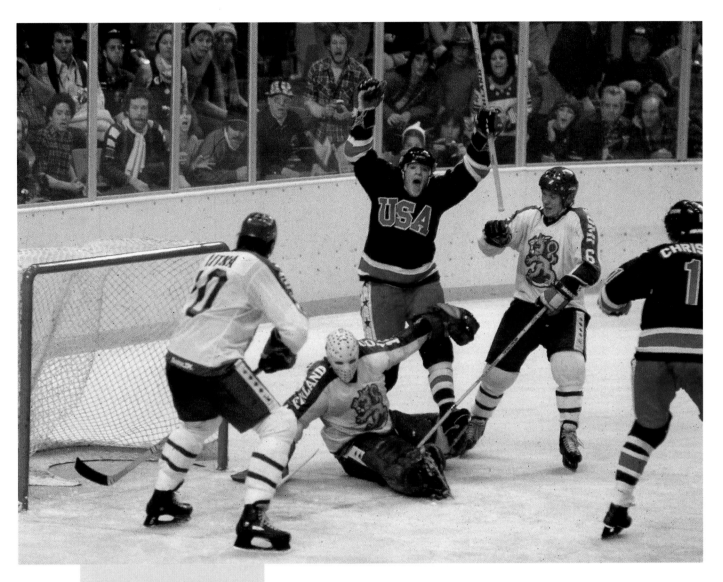

Kluetmeier caught Mark Johnson's ecstatic expression after he scored a goal against Finland.

fired a shot, took the rebound, then shot again for the goal.

With the lead, and with time running out, the fans in the arena sensed victory. "We're number one!" the fans shouted, and soon Team USA was indeed number one, the gold medal winners in hockey at the 1980 Games.

The next day President Carter sent a plane to take the players to the White House. Carter knew they were heroes and how proud the country was of them. "Their victory,"

he said at a White House ceremony, "was one of the most breathtaking upsets, not only in Olympic history but in the entire history of sports." But politics was not far from the celebration, as the president once again called for a boycott of the Summer Games. Goalie Jim Craig joined speed skating hero Eric Heiden in opposing a boycott.

When the ceremony ended, the members of Team USA went their separate ways. Some headed to the NHL, where their victory had a great impact. In the years that followed, team officials were more likely to draft American players, even right out of high school. And kids who might never

Kluetmeier's photo again graced the cover of *Sports Illustrated* when the magazine named the hockey team Sportsmen of the Year.

have laced up skates before wanted to play hockey. Others who already played were inspired to do better. New York Islander great Pat LaFontaine remembered being 16 and watching the Americans win. "I was jumping around the house like crazy," said LaFontaine. "I said to myself, 'God, I want to be one of those guys.'" And he became one, playing on the 1984 U.S. national team. LaFontaine went on to become just the third U.S. player to score 1,000 points in the NHL. He was inducted into the Hockey Hall of Fame in 2003.

At the end of 1980, Heinz Kluetmeier's picture of the Americans celebrating their Miracle on Ice once again appeared on the cover of *Sports Illustrated*. This time the photo was framed by an image of the team's gold medals. The cover recognized Team USA as the winner of the magazine's Sportsmen of the Year award. It was the first team ever to win the award.

In a *Sports Illustrated* article announcing the honor 10 months after the miracle win, Mark Pavelich said the players had not seen the game as a political contest, even if some Americans had. "The truth of the matter is, it was just a hockey game. There was enough to worry about without worrying about Afghanistan or winning it for the pride and glory of the United States. We wanted to win it for ourselves." But as reporter E. M. Swift wrote, "for two weeks in February they—a bunch of unheralded amateurs—became the best hockey team in the world. The best team. The whole was greater than the sum of

its parts by a mile. And they were not just a team, they were innovative and exuberant and absolutely unafraid to succeed. They were a perfect reflection of how Americans wanted to perceive themselves."

In the world outside hockey, the United States and dozens of other nations boycotted the Summer Games in Moscow. Neither the boycott nor other U.S actions forced the Soviet Union out of Afghanistan. They fought a long and bloody war there for most of the decade. The war played a part in training men who later became terrorists

In the decades
after the
Miracle on Ice,
the world has
changed, but
the impact
of the game
remains.

intent on attacking the United States. The war also helped convince some Soviet leaders that they could not continue the Cold War. The country could not compete in the arms race as it once had and meet the basic needs of its citizens.

An effort to improve relations with the United States started after Mikhail Gorbachev took over the Soviet government in 1985. The next year he and President Ronald Reagan met in Iceland to discuss eliminating large numbers of nuclear weapons. The talks, and actual reductions, continued after George H. W. Bush became president in 1989.

By then, Gorbachev was also making changes within his country. He slowly gave the people more freedom. In 1989 the government let Sergei Pryakhin leave the country to play hockey in the NHL. Others soon followed, including several from the 1980 Olympic team.

The number of Soviet players in the NHL increased after their country's communist government ended in 1991. The country split into 15 separate nations. Most of the players who made it in the NHL were from Russia, as had been true with the old Red Army team. But some also came from Latvia, Ukraine, and other former Soviet republics.

In the decades after the Miracle on Ice, the world has changed, but the impact of the game remains. *Sports Illustrated* asked its readers in 2014 to name the most iconic cover photograph during the magazine's 60-year history. They chose Heinz Kluetmeier's picture of Team

USA celebrating its win over the Soviet Union. In the years after the Lake Placid Games, Kluetmeier covered Winter and Summer Olympics around the world.

ANOTHER FAMOUS SHOT

Kluetmeier's photo showed Michael Phelps (left) winning Olympic gold by one-hundredth of a second.

Heinz Kluetmeier has seen some changes in how photographers are allowed to work at the Olympics. During the 1972 Summer Games in Munich, he and the other photographers covering swimming events had to stay in a balcony above the pool. They had to get special permission to be closer to the action when American swimmer Mark Spitz won his record seventh gold medal of the games.

Twenty years later Kluetmeier got much closer to the action—and made sports photography history. He was able to put a camera underwater during the Summer Olympics in Barcelona, Spain. Using a fish-eye lens, he was able to shoot American swimmer Mel Stewart winning the gold medal in the 200-meter butterfly, while also capturing the scoreboard above the pool, the stands, and the blue sky.

But Kluetmeier's most famous underwater shot came at the 2008 Olympic Games in Beijing, China. Using a remote-controlled camera, he took a series of pictures that showed American Michael Phelps coming from behind at the last instant to win the gold in the 100-meter butterfly. Kluetmeier said it was "not a pretty stroke picture, but it is a wonderful journalistic moment to show winning and losing of that particular race."

Still, Kluetmeier could not always get the shots he wanted. At the 2010 Winter Games in Vancouver, officials limited his access to certain events. At those games, Kluetmeier was once again by the ice, photographing hockey action for *Sports Illustrated*.

Goalie Jim Craig
and defenseman
Ken Morrow
defended the net
in an action-packed
Kluetmeier photo
from the 1980
miracle game.

Kluetmeier captured many great moments. But he agreed that the Miracle on Ice shot was the most memorable Olympic photo he ever took.

In 2007 Kluetmeier won the Lucie Award, given to the best photographers, for his achievement in sports photography. He said that to him, the essence of being

Kluetmeier has shot more than 100 cover photos for *Sports Illustrated*.

a good sports photographer is "to have a vision, to have an emotional feeling, to care about what you're photographing, and to have something that's already there in your heart, in your eye." Kluetmeier also saw himself as a journalist with a camera. He took photographs that told a story. His Miracle on Ice photo told the story of victory, the players' joy, and the pride of the fans in the stands.

The 1980 gold-medal achievement has also been the subject of several films. One appeared on TV the next year. HBO showed a documentary in 2001, and three years later

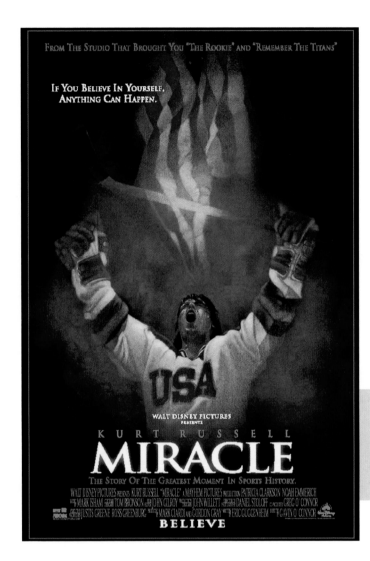

the Walt Disney company released *Miracle,* a feature film starring Kurt Russell as Herb Brooks.

Former goalie Vladislav Tretiak saw *Miracle,* and he said he enjoyed it. In a 2010 interview at the Vancouver Olympics he said, "I applaud the Americans for making a very nice movie ... very patriotic and very good for kids. The memories came back to me."

By then, Tretiak and the other former Soviet players had put the stinging loss behind them. Their team had gone on to win gold medals in the next two Olympics, in 1984 and 1988. But as late as 2006, defenseman Valeri Vasiliev was still calling the game "a Mirage on Ice." He said, "I still can't understand how we could have lost to the Americans. I still can't believe in that—as if it were a dream."

Tretiak, though, had a different perspective several years later. He said before the start of the 2014 Winter Games in Sochi, Russia, "In 1980, it was a good lesson that the Americans taught us. You have to respect your competitors and only after the game can you tell what you think about them. We did not have respect for the competitors at that time, and that's why we lost."

For the American players, the glow of the Miracle on Ice did not fade. In 2015, to mark the 35th anniversary of the game, all surviving members of the team went back to the arena in Lake Placid. It was their first time together since 1980. (Bob Suter had died the year before). The arena where they achieved their miracle is now named for Herb Brooks. The team, along with 5,000 fans, watched a tape of their victory over the Soviet Union.

Mark Ramsey, the youngest player on the team, summed up what he and other players felt. "It's amazing the staying power this has had. Obviously, we knew we were onto something big. But we had no idea it was going to a grab a country like it did. No idea."

The Miracle on Ice did grab a country, one that wanted winners and heroes. And one picture captured that historic moment forever.

LIFE AFTER THE OLYMPICS

Team USA's 1980 Olympic win made the 20 young men American heroes. But for them life soon returned to normal. Many pursued careers in the NHL. Others stayed active in hockey in other ways. Here are some of their achievements after the 1980 Games:

• Defenseman Bill Baker of the University of Minnesota played three seasons in the NHL before becoming an oral surgeon.

• Center Neal Broten of the University of Minnesota scored more than 900 points in his career and helped the New Jersey Devils win the 1995 Stanley Cup, the trophy given to the league's champions.

• Right wing Dave Christian of the University of North Dakota played in the NHL for 15 seasons, scoring a career-best 41 goals in 1985–86. His father and two uncles were also Olympic hockey players.

• Center Steve Christoff of the University of Minnesota played in the NHL for five years before pursuing a career as a pilot.

• Goalie Jim Craig of Boston University played in 30 NHL games before beginning a career in sales and marketing. He now speaks across the country to help others achieve their goals.

• Left wing Mike Eruzione of Boston University played his last hockey game in the 1980 Olympics and then became a TV broadcaster. He works for Boston University and gives speeches to motivate others to succeed.

• Right wing John Harrington of the University of Minnesota-Duluth played several more seasons for the U.S. national hockey team before beginning a career as a coach and NHL scout. He coaches the women's hockey team at Minnesota State University, Mankato.

• Backup goalie Steve Janaszak of the University of Minnesota played in three NHL games and then started a career in finance.

• Center Mark Johnson of the University of Wisconsin played for five NHL teams before coaching college hockey. He coaches the University of Wisconsin women's team. He coached the U.S. women's team to a silver medal in the 2010 Olympics.

• Defenseman Ken Morrow of Bowling Green State University helped the New York Islanders win four consecutive Stanley Cups and continued to work for the team after he retired as a player.

• Left wing Rob McClanahan of the University of Minnesota played five years in the NHL and then went into finance.

• Defenseman Jack O'Callahan of Boston University played seven seasons in the pros and then started a career in finance.

• Center Mark Pavelich of the University of Minnesota-Duluth averaged almost a point a game during his seven-year NHL career. He also played several seasons in Europe.

• Defenseman Mike Ramsey of the University of Minnesota played professional hockey for 18 years and appeared in four NHL All-Star games before becoming a coach.

• Left wing William "Buzz" Schneider of the University of Minnesota played hockey in Europe before beginning a real estate career in the United States.

• Right wing Dave Silk of Boston University played professsionally in both North America and Europe and also coached in the college ranks.

• Right wing Eric Strobel of the University of Minnesota suffered an ankle injury that ended his dream of making the NHL. He later went into business.

• Defenseman Bob Suter of the University of Wisconsin opened a sporting goods store and was working as a scout for the Minnesota Wild professional hockey team when he died in 2014. His son Ryan, also an Olympian, plays for the Wild.

• Left wing Phil Verchota of the University of Minnesota played for Team USA during the 1984 Winter Games and then became a banker.

• Center Mark Wells of Bowling Green State University was drafted by the Montreal Canadiens but never played in the NHL. He worked for a time in the restaurant business but had to retire because of a spinal disease.

Members of the 1980 hockey team lit the flame at the 2002 Winter Olympics in Salt Lake City, Utah.

Timeline

1956

The Soviet Union's hockey team wins its first Olympic gold medal at the Winter Games in Cortina, Italy; the United States wins the silver medal

1960

The U.S. team wins its first hockey Olympic gold medal at the Winter Games in Squaw Valley, California; Canada wins the silver medal and the Soviets win the bronze

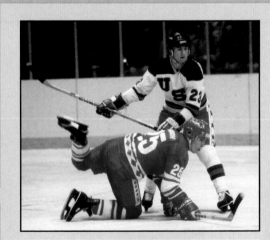

January 1980

President Jimmy Carter calls for a boycott of the 1980 Summer Olympics in Moscow

February 9, 1980

In their last game before the Olympics, the Americans lose 10-3 to the Soviets

1964

The Soviet Union wins hockey gold, beginning a medal domination that will last nearly 30 years; the Soviets will go on to win seven gold medals in eight tries

1979

Herb Brooks begins recruiting and training players for the 1980 U.S. hockey team; the Soviet Union invades Afghanistan in December

February 22, 1980

In the biggest upset in international hockey history, the Americans defeat the Soviets in the semifinals of the Olympics for a "Miracle on Ice"

February 24, 1980

Team USA defeats Finland to win the Olympic gold medal at Lake Placid, New York

Timeline

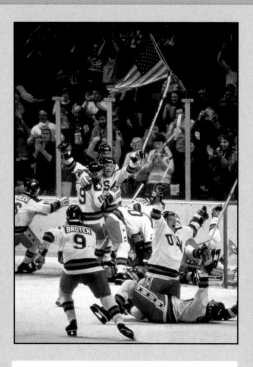

1980

Heinz Kluetmeier's photo of the Miracle on Ice celebration appears twice on the cover of *Sports Illustrated,* in March and December

1986

Soviet leader Mikhail Gorbachev and President Ronald Reagan hold their first direct talks to discuss eliminating some of their nuclear weapons

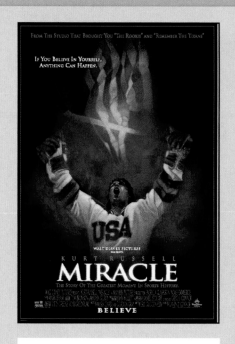

2004

The Walt Disney movie *Miracle* tells the story of the 1980 U.S. Olympic hockey team

1989

Sergei Pryakhin is the first Soviet player allowed to join the NHL

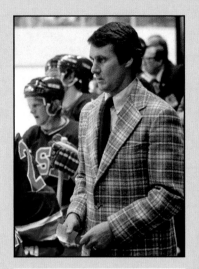

August 11, 2003

Coach Herb Brooks dies in a car accident north of Minneapolis, Minnesota

2014

Readers of *Sports Illustrated* name Kluetmeier's cover photo of the Miracle on Ice celebration the most memorable in the magazine's 60-year history

2015

On the 35th anniversary of the Miracle on Ice, the surviving members of the 1980 team reunite at Lake Placid

Glossary

blue lines—two lines that extend across the ice 60 feet
(18 meters) from each goal; they divide the ice into attacking,
neutral, and defending zones

boards—wooden or fiberglass wall that surrounds the rink to
keep the puck and players inside the rink; shatter-resistant glass
above the boards helps to protect spectators from flying pucks

boycott—to refuse to buy or use a product or service or to
participate in an event to protest something believed to be
wrong or unfair

capitalism—economic system that allows people to freely
create businesses and own as much property as they can afford

check—contact by a defending player against an opponent to
get the puck away from him or slow him down; only allowed
against a player in control of the puck or against the last player
to control it immediately after he gives it up

communism—system in which goods and property are owned
by the government and shared in common; Communist rulers
limit personal freedoms to achieve their goals

face-off—dropping the puck between two players, one from
each team, to start or resume play

freeze—to hold the puck against the boards with a stick
or skate to force the referee to briefly stop play

iconic—widely viewed as perfectly capturing the meaning
or spirit of something or someone

power play—occurs when a team has a one- or two-player
advantage because of the oppenent's penalties

shot on goal—when a player shoots the puck with the
intention of scoring, but only if the shot would have gone in
the net had the goalie not stopped it

Additional Resources

Further Reading

Bearce, Stephanie. *The Cold War: Secrets, Special Missions, and Hidden Facts About the CIA, KGB, and MI6*. Top Secret Files. Waco, Texas: Prufrock Press Inc., 2015.

Hunter, Nick. *The Winter Olympics*.
Chicago: Heinemann Library, 2014.

Winters, Jaime. *Breakaway! The History of Hockey*.
New York: Crabtree Publishing Company, 2015.

Internet Sites

Use FactHound to find Internet sites related to this book. All of the sites on FactHound have been researched by our staff.

Here's all you do:
Visit *www.facthound.com*
Type in this code: 9780756552909

Critical Thinking Using the Common Core

The United States was facing problems leading up to the 1980 Winter Olympics. How did Team USA's miracle win help change the country's mood? Would a similar sports win today help boost morale in the United States? (Integration of Knowledge and Ideas)

How did Soviet coach Anatoly Tarasov transform how hockey players trained and played? (Key Ideas and Details)

Look at the images on pages 20 and 31. What are some ways that hockey has changed through the years? (Craft and Structure)

Source Notes

Page 6, line 20: Wayne Coffey. *The Boys of Winter: The Untold Story of a Coach, a Dream, and the 1980 U.S. Olympic Hockey Team*. New York: Crown Publishers, 2005, p. 230.

Page 10, line 1: Ibid., p. 37.

Page 12, line 10: Ibid, p. 237.

Page 12, line 12: Ibid., p. 238.

Page 12, line 22: Joe Posnanski. "10 interesting facts you may not know about the Miracle on Ice." *Sports Illustrated*. 22 Feb. 2010. 22 June 2015. http://www.si.com/more-sports/2010/02/22/miracle-onice

Page 17, line 7: Frederick T. Birchall. "Visitors to Olympics Carrying Away Highly Favorable Impression of Reich." *The New York Times*. Sports, p. S2. 16 Aug. 1936. 22 June 2015. http://query.nytimes.com/gst/abstract.html?res=9A03EFD8173DE33BBC4E52DFBE66838D629EDE

Page 21, line 2: Ronald Sullivan. "Anatoly Tarasov, 76, Innovative Coach of Hockey in Soviet Union." *The New York Times*. 24 June 1995. 22 June 2015. http://www.nytimes.com/1995/06/24/obituaries/anatoly-tarasov-76-innovative-coach-of-hockey-in-soviet-union.html?pagewanted=print

Page 22, line 7: *Red Army*. A film by Gabe Polsky. Sony Pictures Classics, 2015.

Page 25, line 1: John Kreiser. "1972 Summit Series Shaped Modern Hockey." NHL.com. 1 Sept. 2012. 23 June 2015. http://www.nhl.com/ice/news.htm?id=640724

Page 26, line 23: *The Boys of Winter*, p. 9.

Page 26, line 26: Ibid.

Page 27, col. 1, line 14: Herb Brooks Quotes. Herb Brooks Foundation. 23 June 2015. http://www.herbbrooksfoundation.com/page/show/740804-herb-brooks-quotes

Page 29, line 3: Lawrie Mifflin. "Soviet icemen deflate USA amateurs 10-3." *New York Daily News*. 10 Feb. 1980. 22 June 2015. http://www.nydailynews.com/sports/hockey/russians-easy-u-s-olympians-fall-10-3-article-1.2023417

Page 31, line 4: *The Boys of Winter*, p. 98.

Page 32, line 9: Herb Brooks Quotes.

Page 33, line 7: *The Boys of Winter*, p. 74.

Page 34, line 4: Associated Press. "Olympic greats Tretiak, Rodnina light cauldron." *Daily Mail*. 7 Feb. 2014. 22 June 2015. http://www.dailymail.co.uk/wires/ap/article-2554165/Olympic-greats-Tretiak-Rodnina-light-cauldron.html

Page 35, col. 1, line 6: "U.S. Defeat Soviet Squad in Olympic Hockey by 4-3." *The New York Times*, p. 16. 23 Feb. 1980. 23 June 2015. http://timesmachine.nytimes.com/timesmachine/1980/02/23/112052597.html?pageNumber=16

Page 35, col. 1, line 10: *The Boys of Winter*, p. 91.

Page 35, col. 2, line 6: Kevin Allen. "College Kids Perform Olympic Miracle." ESPN Classic. 23 June 2015. https://espn.go.com/classic/s/miracle_ice_1980.html

Page 35, col.2, line 8: *The Boys of Winter*, p. 91.

Page 41, line 4: Jack DeGange. "A Snapshot in Time." *Dartmouth Big Green*. 6 Nov. 2007. 22 June 2015. http://www.dartmouthsports.com/ViewArticle.dbml?DB_OEM_ID=11600&ATCLID=1305347

Page 41, line 16: "10 Interesting facts you may not know about the Miracle on Ice."

Page 41, line 23: Robert D. McFadden. "Cheers Resound Across Nation." *The New York Times*. Sports, p. 16. 23 Feb. 1980. 23 June 2015. http://timesmachine.nytimes.com/timesmachine/1980/02/23/issue.html

Page 43, line 8: Steven R. Weisman. "Olympians, Welcomed by Carter, Offer Petition Opposing a Boycott." *The New York Times*, p. C11. 26 Feb. 1980. 23 June 2015. http://timesmachine.nytimes.com/timesmachine/1980/02/26/112054808.html?pageNumber=47

Page 45, line 4: Jack Friedman. "1980's 'Miracle on Ice' Gives Hockey Coach Lou Vairo An Extremely Tough Act to Follow." *People*. 12 Dec. 1983. 23 June 2015. http://www.people.com/people/archive/article/0,,20086563,00.html

Page 45, line 21: E.M. Swift. "A Reminder Of What We Can Be: The 1980 U.S. Olympic Hockey Team." *Sports Illustrated*. 22–29 Dec. 1980. 23 June 2015. http://www.si.com/olympic-ice-hockey/2014/10/28/reminder-what-we-can-be-1980-us-olympic-hockey-team-si-60

Page 45, line 26: Ibid.

Page 49, col. 2, line 7: Richard Deitsch. "Q&A with SI's Heinz Kluetmeier." *Sports Illustrated*. 19 Aug. 2008. 23 June 2015. http://www.si.com/more-sports/2008/08/19/heinz-qanda

Page 51, line 1: Heinz Kluetmeier. The Lucie Awards. 23 June 2015. http://www.lucies.org/honorees/heinz-kluetmeier/

Page 52, line 5: Associated Press. "'Miracle on Ice': Both sides recall U.S.A.'s momentous 1980 hockey upset win over the Soviet Union." Cleveland.com. 21 Feb. 2010. 23 June 2015. http://www.cleveland.com/olympics/index.ssf/2010/02/miracle_on_ice_both_sides_reca.html

Page 53, line 3: Ibid.

Page 53, line 9: Mark Kiszla. "Russian Pride is Betting Big on its Hockey Team." *The Denver Post*. 2 Dec. 2014. 23 June 2015. http://www.denverpost.com/ci_25119082/kiszla-russian-pride-is-betting-big-its-hockey

Page 53, line 23: Scott Burnside. "'Miracle' Team Revels in Reunion." ESPN.com. 23 Feb. 2015. 23 June 2015. http://espn.go.com/nhl/story/_/id/12369606/nhl-miracle-ice-35th-anniversary-brings-back-memories-all-involved

Select Bibliography

Allen, Kevin. "College Kids Perform Olympic Miracle." ESPN Classic. https://espn.go.com/classic/s/miracle_ice_1980.html

Allen, Kevin. "The First Miracle on Ice." ESPN Classic. https://espn.go.com/classic/s/1960_ice_mircle_1226.html

"Anatoly Tarasov—The Father of Soviet Ice Hockey." The Voice of Russia. 2 June 2008. 23 June 2015. http://sputniknews.com/voiceofrussia/2008/06/02/196349/

Coffey, Wayne. The Boys of Winter: The Untold Story of a Coach, a Dream, and the 1980 U.S. Olympic Hockey Team. New York: Crown Publishers, 2005.

DeGange, Jack. "A Snapshot in Time." Dartmouth Big Green. 6 Nov. 2007. 23 June 2015. http://www.dartmouthsports.com/ViewArticle.dbml?DB_OEM_ID=11600&ATCLID=1305347

Deitsch, Richard. "Q&A with SI's Heinz Kluetmeier." Sports Illustrated. 19 Aug. 2008. 23 June 2015. http://www.si.com/more-sports/2008/08/19/heinz-qanda

Do You Believe in Miracles? The Story of the 1980 U.S. Olympic Hockey Team. HBO, 2001.

Eskenazi, Gerald. "U.S. Defeat Soviet Squad in Olympic Hockey by 4-3." The New York Times, p. 16. 23 Feb. 1980. 23 June 2015. http://timesmachine.nytimes.com/timesmachine/1980/02/23/112052597.html?pageNumber=16

Forgotten Miracle. Golden Puck Pictures, 2009.

Gilbert, John. Herb Brooks: The Inside Story of a Hockey Mastermind. Minneapolis: MBI Publishing Co., 2008.

Gordon, Stefanie. "Poignant Reunion for the Miracle on Ice Team at Lake Placid." Sports Illustrated. 23 Feb. 2015. 23 June 2015. http://www.si.com/nhl/2015/02/23/1980-usa-olympic-hockey-team-miracle-on-ice-35th-reunion-at-lake-placid

Guttmann, Allen. "The Cold War and the Olympics." International Journal. Vol. 43, No. 4, Sport in World Politics, Autumn 1988, pp. 554–568.

Heinz Kluetmeier. The Lucie Awards. http://www.lucies.org/honorees/heinz-kluetmeier/

Jones, Meg. "Photographer Kluetmeier Remembers Angles of Olympics' Big Moments." Milwaukee Journal Sentinel. 15 March 2010. 23 June 2015. http://www.jsonline.com/news/milwaukee/87726722.html

Kaplan, Michael. "Masters of Olympic Photography: Heinz Kluetmeier." American Photo. 27 July 2012. 23 June 2015. http://www.americanphotomag.com/masters-olympic-photography-heinz-kluetmeier

Kimball, Bob. "Eye-opener: 'Miracle on Ice' big part of politics-sports collision." USA Today. 22 Feb. 2010. 23 June 2015. http://content.usatoday.com/communities/gameon/post/2010/02/eye-opener-the-good-old-hockey-game-then-and-now/1#.VUo-i_m6eUk

Klein, Jeff Z. "It's Not Hockey, It's Bandy." The New York Times. 28 Jan. 2010. 23 June 2015. http://www.nytimes.com/2010/01/29/sports/olympics/29bandy.html?_r=2&ref=sports

Leffler, Melvyn P. For the Soul of Mankind: The United States, the Soviet Union, and the Cold War. New York: Hill and Wang, 2007.

McFadden, Robert D. "Cheers Resound Across Nation." The New York Times. Sports, p. 16. 23 Feb. 1980. 23 June 2015. http://timesmachine.nytimes.com/timesmachine/1980/02/23/issue.html

Mifflin, Lawrie. "Soviet icemen deflate USA amateurs 10-3." New York Daily News. 10 Feb. 1980. 23 June 2015. http://www.nydailynews.com/sports/hockey/russians-easy-u-s-olympians-fall-10-3-article-1.2023417

Mifflin, Lawrie. "U.S. hockey team completes the Miracle on Ice with 4-2 win over Finland for Olympic gold." New York Daily News. 25 Feb. 1980. 23 June 2015. http://www.nydailynews.com/sports/hockey/no-1-article-1.2030322

Miracle. Buena Vista Home Entertainment, 2004.

Of Miracles and Men. ESPN, 2015.

Posnanski, Joe. "10 interesting facts you may not know about the Miracle on Ice." Sports Illustrated. 22 Feb. 2010. 23 June 2015. http://www.si.com/more-sports/2010/02/22/miracle-onice

Red Army. A film by Gabe Polsky. Sony Pictures Classics, 2015.

Reid, Kirsty. "Blood in the water: Hungary's 1956 water polo gold." BBC News. 20 Aug. 2011. 23 June 2015. http://www.bbc.com/news/world-14575260

Sandomir, Richard. "How 'Miracle on Ice' Helped Restore Faith." The New York Times. 2 Feb. 2001. 23 June 2015. http://www.nytimes.com/2001/02/02/sports/tv-sports-how-miracle-on-ice-helped-restore-faith.html

Sarantakes, Nicholas Evan. "Jimmy Carter's Disastrous Olympic Boycott." Politico Magazine. 9 Feb. 2014. 23 June 2015. http://www.politico.com/magazine/story/2014/02/carter-olympic-boycott-1980-103308.html#.VUpGxvm6eUl

Sullivan, Ronald. "Anatoly Tarasov, 76, Innovative Coach of Hockey in Soviet Union." The New York Times. 24 June 1995. 23 June 2015. http://www.nytimes.com/1995/06/24/obituaries/anatoly-tarasov-76-innovative-coach-of-hockey-in-soviet-union.html?pagewanted=print

Swift, E.M. "A Reminder Of What We Can Be: The 1980 U.S. Olympic Hockey Team." Sports Illustrated. 22–29 Dec. 1980. 23 June 2015. http://www.si.com/olympic-ice-hockey/2014/10/28/reminder-what-we-can-be-1980-us-olympic-hockey-team-si-60

Swift, E.M. "Miracle on Ice." Sports Illustrated. 3 March 1980. 23 June 2015. http://www.si.com/sports-illustrated/2014/08/15/si-vault-miracle-ice

"U.S.A. Beats Soviet Union in 'Miracle on Ice.'" The New York Times Learning Network. 22 Feb. 2012. 23 June 2015. http://learning.blogs.nytimes.com/2012/02/22/feb-22-1980-u-s-a-beats-soviet-union-in-miracle-on-ice/?_r=2

Index

About the Author

Michael Burgan has written many books for children and young adults during his 20 years as a freelance writer. Most of his books have focused on history. Burgan has won several awards for his writing. He lives in Santa Fe, New Mexico.